Abandoned by the Muse
A Bundle of Poetry

Bieke Stengos

Vocamus Press | Guelph, Ontario

Written by Bieke Stengos
Some rights reserved
©⊕⊛⊜

ISBN 13: 978-0-9881049-7-6 (pbk)
ISBN 13: 978-0-9881049-8-3 (ebk)

Vocamus Press
130 Dublin Street, North
Guelph, Ontario, Canada
N1H 4N4

www.vocamus.net

2014

For my children, who are my home
For Thanasi, who takes me away from it

Abandoned by the Muse
A Bundle of Poetry

Bieke Stengos

Autumn

I

When I first ventured onto the path of love
My head on his shoulder
Your hand reaching for mine
Home was no more
Than a bare mattress on a barren floor
Where used tissues lay scattered
Like magnolia blossoms

You showed me
How one thing fit into another
How patterns
Are woven all around us

When you drew me close
I turned away from him
And when I looked back
He was already gone

Tears collected in the palm of my hand
Even while your spirit ran empty into mine
It was then
Words rearranged themselves
It was then you gave me life

II

In those days
That stretched like lazy cats
Tails counting out seconds
I was the line
From your hand
To empty canvas

I lived as if you would always perch
On the crest of my mind
Until the fire of the autumn sun
Left only dry leaves
To fall silent
Underneath the crunch of our feet

When night came without warning
You fluttered with the leaves
Burning against a darkening sky

I drove through a line of time
Where rainbows splashed colours
Onto the blank page before me

III

He left me
A widow without a ring
You left me nothing but
A heart
Without crying

And I spend my time
crafting empty words
To give meaning
To an empty mind

IV

I woke in the dead of night
The memory of your breath
No longer on my cheek
And people
Like rotten meat
Lying by the wayside

I ran through empty streets
Begging for tears
Calling for danger
I screamed with a mouth gaping wide
as black-winged creatures
feasted on this human mess

I beseeched the bird of paradise
To swoop down from the heavens
I appealed to archangels
I squabbled with the many-coloured seraphim
But none could penetrate
The great white mantel
That shrouds you

V

Still reaching for you through rings of fire
I dwelled within the great white circle
Where you filled me with light
But when I learned to draw
A line that reached
For celestial beings
They spread their wings wide
To hide you from my world-worn eyes

As the sun carved growing shadows
I searched for you among sages and wise men
Among painters and poets
I looked for you in the turn of a phrase
In the light behind a line
In the truth behind a lie

I thought I'd find you
In luring eyes
But when I lost you
In the shrug of a shoulder
I shredded white paper
And hurled the pieces towards the sky

VI

Toothless grins on pumpkins
Against the dappled chill of clouds
The monotony of cut cornstalks
No, I am not ready yet
I am not done
Winter is still too far away

So I look for you
Whenever the sun strikes the last struggle of green
I call for you against the stretch of a stripped tree
I find you in the rustle of that forgotten cornfield
And I lose you again in the loop of a willow bough
Where I abandon you
To the last warm rays
Of a sun that keeps on flashing by

VII

The warmth of summer
Died with a slight
Hesitation from your hand
Gulls rise in trails
Of shiver and sway

Can't you see
How the upturned earth
Raw, open, dank
Is ready
For the cover of snow

This dying game
Has left me
Little hope
That spring
Will return again

VIII

While I search in vain
For winter's blanket
The sun persists
In its seduction
Of birds and unsuspecting buds
Clouds trail airy wisps
Over comfortable cows
That chew the cud
Among fresh shoots
In the dying grass

O joy of spring
My heart exclaims
Have you returned to us so soon

IX

Softness like spring
Over a waiting field
No scars
Only the sun with a tender veil of care
Has me fooled
O blue sky
O sunshine
O time long past
When the expression of emotion
Did not need a mask
When poets could sigh alas and alack
When the black of a creeping branch
On rust-coloured grass could sigh along
With the droop of a tree
And weep with the light
Behind a single blade of grass

If not for the rational mind
I could almost believe
That the final season
Would not descend

Winter

X

Sunlight filters
Through slender trees
That harbour secret places
The first pinpricks of winter
Assault me
With a promise that nothing
Will lay waste forever

XI

Organ music
Shatters the light
Into a latticework of clouds
That tumbles down
To a fallen tree
Lying silent
Like a child's fear
When her father strikes the person
She loves most

XII

Rows of trees reflected
In the glaze of snow
Stand sentinel
To a tidy little world
That we pretend
Is whole

XIII

Black ice
Sharp cornered slabs
Flying shards of glass
And the rest of it
The woods
The fields
The white-brown shoulder of the road
So still

XIV

When I dream you into being
I find myself lost in a fog-invaded forest
Of glimmering naked trees
That rise
from the blue-white snow
Cold like your body
Before heat devoured it

I search for a place to breathe freely
But I get lost
In the press of your lips
Against the stretched skin of time
And the memory of you fading
Like a melting negative
Of a city with no sun
Where streets run dead into low walls

When I open my eyes
To a black line of upright trees
I vanish from sight

    – For Sara

XV

Sunlight flees over an open field
Like a fugitive striving to pass unseen
Whirls of dust fly high
Cars are left
Stranded by the side of the road
The landscape is losing its depth
It turns pale blue
With lines lost in stubby remains
Of a mowed down cornfield
There is no freeze to cut the pain
No storm to celebrate
The rage when I realize
This journey from life to death
Is unrelenting

XVI

When my breath paints gossamer on frozen grass
Silent trees turn the landscape black
There is no escape
From the glare of sun
While angels fade
at the horizon
Angels with white golden coats
Imprinted on a barren field

When the world stops turning
I am back to where
Your absence
Betrays me like the clatter of sunlight
On the frozen landscape

No Spring

XVII

I met a woman
She was unable to mourn
The lover who had died too soon

I met a woman
She cried for lovers who left
For happier lives

I met a woman
She died at the hands
Of her mother's words

I met another
Who cried at the sight
Of her baby's swollen belly

Then I found the woman who vowed
That she would never again venture
Onto the path of love
And I picked myself up

XVIII

When I come home
My children run to me
With plump kisses
To wet my cheeks
And I fall back
My arms full of delight

Then morning breaks
In smiles and dimples
And I see
How full of promise
Life can be
When your line of vision
Is the tremble
Of a knee

XIX

Angels on my baby's bowl
Angels on the telly
Cherubs tumbling on my lawn

Behind them
Brushstrokes of goldenrod
And trees ablaze

With arms held high
I reach for the blue sky

Until –you're gone–
Hits me full in the face
And like the burning leaves
I fall from grace

XX

I always thought deep in the mind of me
That I could do it once
And then go back and do it all over
That my child now grown
could restore lost time

I always thought I could stand still forever
But then I remembered
The first time you guided my hand

So let the heat rise
Let the hair fall grey over my forehead
Let the years roll by
But never let the longing cease
That was born in me
The day I met you

XXI

The fields lie waiting
Beneath still air
A red-winged blackbird
Makes an early return

Its stain
A dagger

XXII

You are in the corny radio song
The exuberant speed of the road
The tender expanse of blue sky
The flaming tops of trees
Stretching to come alive

XXIII

You are in the circle
Of lavender clouds
Reducing trees
To black lace
You are
in the rain
Falling softly
To swift violins

XXIV

I try to hold on
To the warm sand
That runs slowly
From the cradle
Of my hand
The memory of you
Lies buried deep
Within me

Acknowledgements

I would like to thank the following people for their invaluable feedback: Robin Downey, Rob O'Flanagan, and Michelle McMillan. I also want to give a special thank you to Jeremy Luke Hill for his insightful critique and his gentle encouragement.

About the Author

Bieke Stengos was born in Flanders, Belgium. She emigrated to Canada and now lives in Guelph, Ontario, with her family. She has published short stories and poems, has finished a first novel, and is working on a second one. *Abandoned by the Muse* is her second book of poetry. The first, *Transmigrator*, was published by The Private Press.

www.ingramcontent.com/pod-product-compliance
Lightning Source LLC
Chambersburg PA
CBHW020021050426
42450CB00005B/587